The Bug

by Mary Alice Cooper
illustrated by Janee Trasler

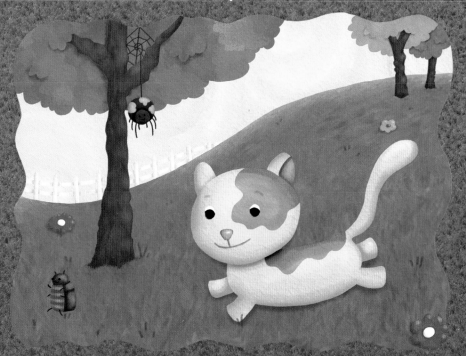

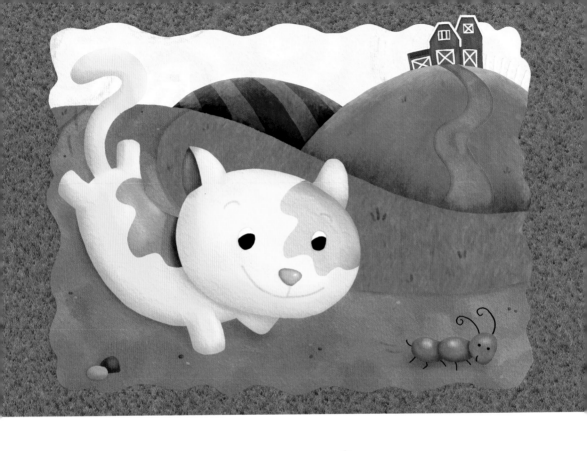

See the 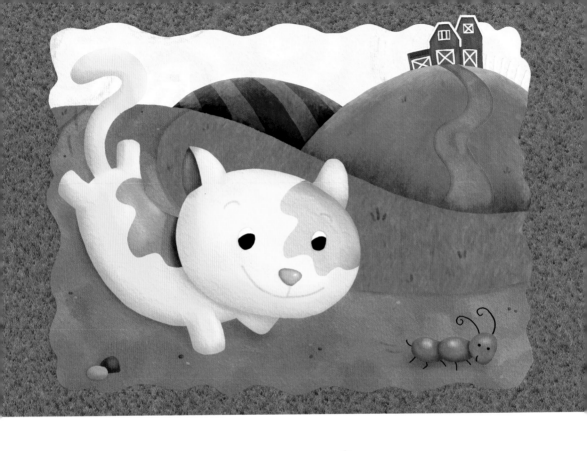 run.

ant

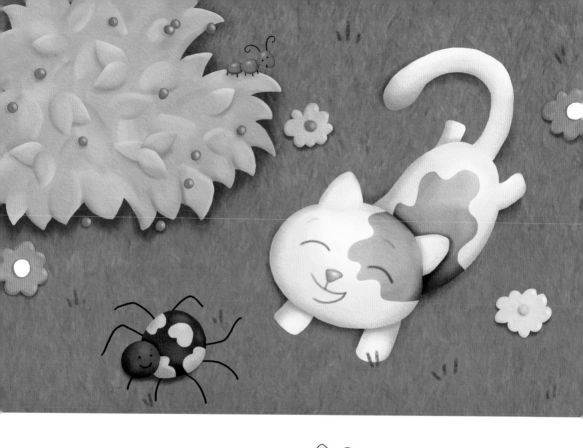

See the 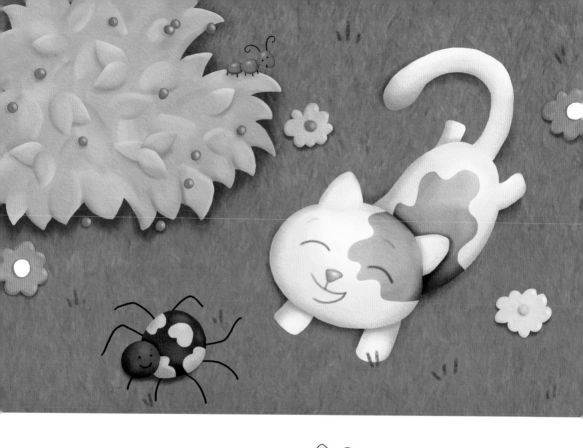 run.

spider

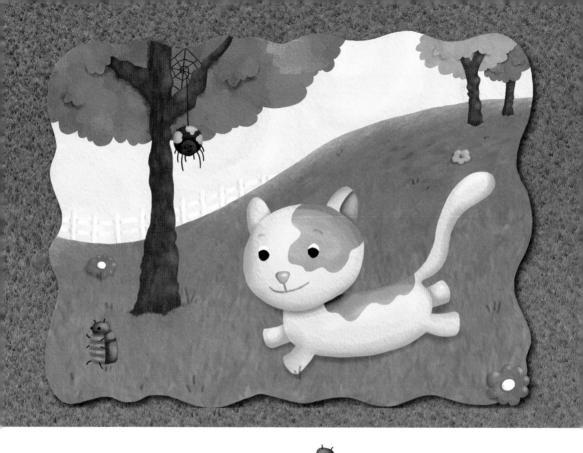

See the 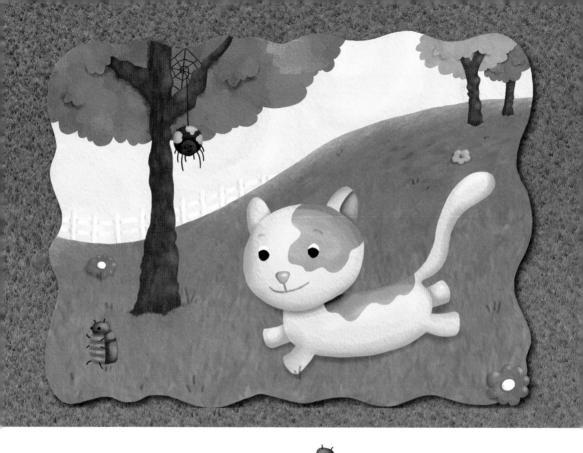 run.

beetle

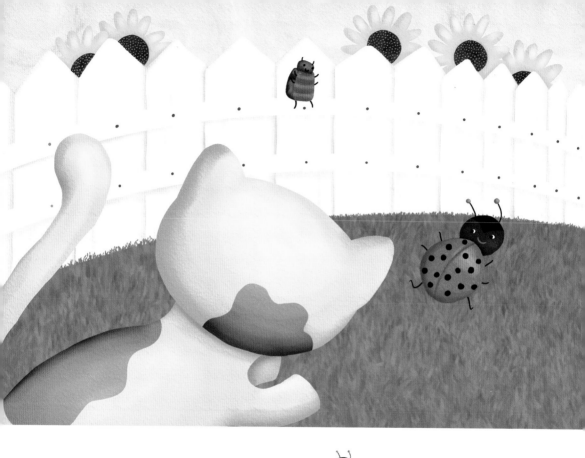

See the 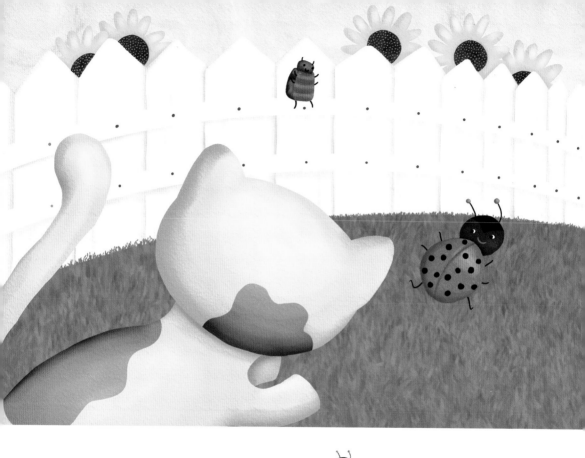 run.
ladybug

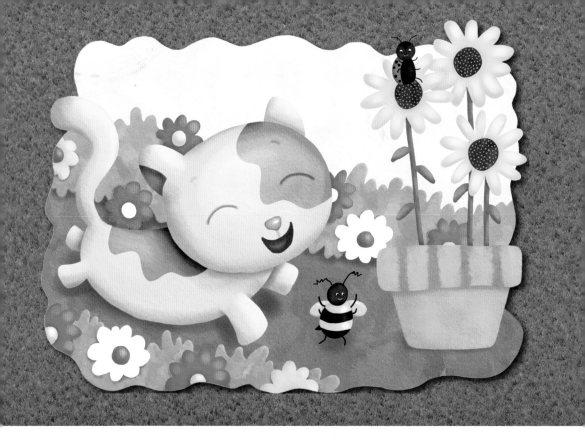

See the run.
bee

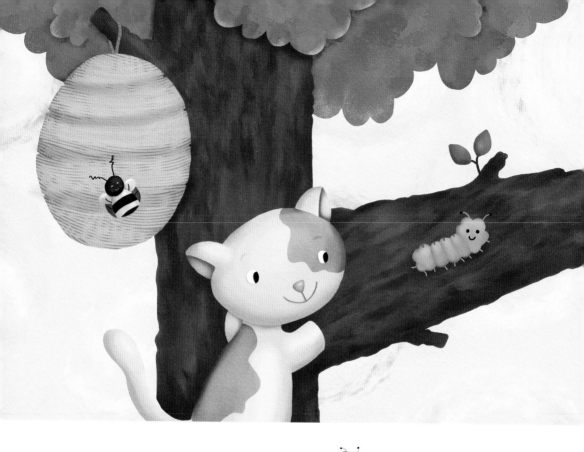

See the 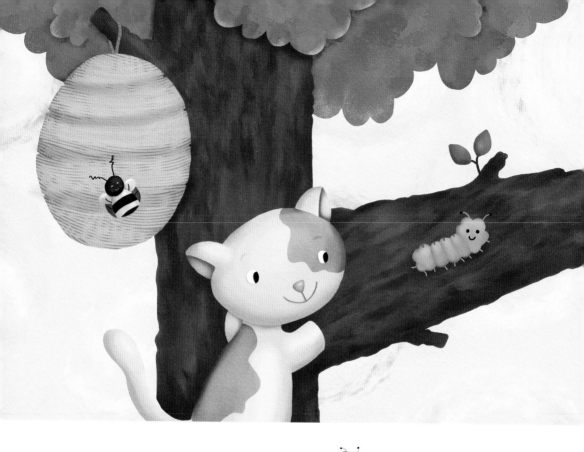 run.

caterpillar

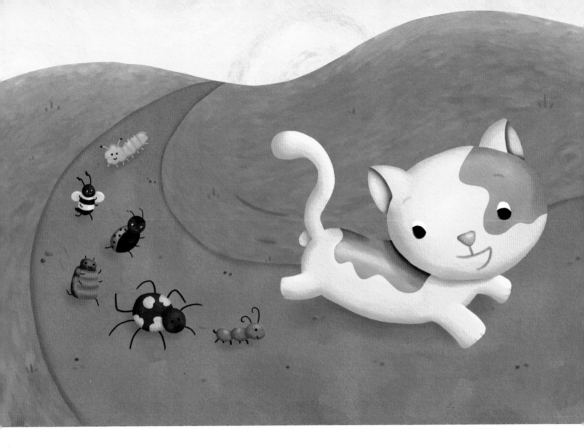

See the run.

kitten